The Assessment and Evaluation of Training

Financial Times Management Briefings are happy to receive proposals from individuals who have expertise in the field of management education.

If you would like to discuss your ideas further, please contact Andrew Mould, Commissioning Editor.

Tel: 0171 447 2210
Fax: 0171 240 5771
e-mail: andrew.mould@pitmanpub.co.uk

FINANCIAL TIMES
Management Briefings

Human Resources

The Assessment and Evaluation of Training

IAN PEARCE

FT PITMAN PUBLISHING

London • Hong Kong • Johannesburg • Melbourne • Singapore • Washington DC

PITMAN PUBLISHING
128 Long Acre, London WC2E 9AN
Tel: +44 (0)171 447 2000
Fax: +44 (0)171 240 5771

A Division of Pearson Professional Limited

First published in Great Britain 1997

ISBN 0 273 63195 0

British Library Cataloguing in Publication Data
A CIP catalogue record for this book can be obtained from the British Library.

10 9 8 7 6 5 4 3 2 1

Printed and bound in Great Britain

The Publishers' policy is to use paper manufactured from sustainable forests.

CONTENTS

ABOUT THE AUTHOR

Dr Ian Pearce is currently the Programme Manager for Central and Eastern Europe at Durham University Business School. He holds a mechanical engineering degree and a doctorate in fluid mechanics. His career started in the manufacture of earth moving equipment, and then changed to the chemical industry. After a succession of technical and management positions he was the senior training manager for the Teesside, UK, sites of Imperial Chemical Industries Chemicals & Polymers Ltd for seven years.

Dr Pearce has advised the managers of several independent training organisations, and is a director of a college in Durham. He has been closely involved with the introduction of National Vocational Qualifications in the chemical industry. His period as ICI Teesside Training Manager included one National Training Award and one Regional Award.

If readers of this report wish to contact Dr Pearce his address is as follows.

Dr I D Pearce
Durham University Business School
Mill Hill Lane
Durham DH1 3LB
United Kingdom

Telephone: 0191 374 3380
Fax: 0191 374 4748

International telephone: +44 191 374 3380
International fax: +44 191 374 4748

CHAPTER 1

INTRODUCTION

If we wish to survive and prosper in these ever changing times, we will probably have to improve our existing skills and develop some new ones. This will involve learning. Learning has moved on from the days where it was confined to school children, apprentices and students. Learning is now a life long business as we face new technologies, changing employment patterns and different social situations.

Learning is concerned with acquiring new knowledge, understanding new concepts, developing new skills, or behaving in a changed manner. Learning can be by individuals, families, teams, organisations and even nations. The rate at which we need to learn can be shown by some examples.

- Individuals using microwave cookery.
- Families dealing with the decline in traditional long-term relationships.
- Teams at work becoming more autonomous as supervisors disappear.
- Organisations like Ford moving from 'any colour as long as it's black' to building each car to an individual customer's specification.
- Nations such as Russia going from leading an empire to living with independent neighbouring states.

Whilst much learning can be done without obvious external support, the process can usually be made more effective by asking others to help. This leads us to the idea of training and development. Although training has been introduced as something learners request, there is no denying that a lot of training is more or less forced on to people. Individuals who ask for car driving lessons usually concentrate on getting the most from the driving instructor. On the other hand, in those countries still operating national military service, the basic training is not a matter of choice, and individuals will probably learn only the minimum needed to get by. If there isn't any choice about taking part in company training programmes, this will clearly have implications for the quality of learning.

Whether we think of learning or training, the notion of evaluation will be important. This can tell us if the new skill has been developed, if a certain behaviour has been modified, and if the desired organisational change has been achieved.

There is often confusion about the terms used to describe the evaluation of training. Of course, unless you are really pedantic, it doesn't matter what word is used, providing everyone understands our definitions. You may have come across most of these terms, and I will define them in two groups.

The first group is assessment, validation and examination. These terms imply a checking against standards of specific knowledge, skill, or ability to carry out a task, generally on an individual basis. Although there are examples of self-assessments, someone else usually carries out the assessment. An example would be watching someone carrying out part of a job and checking that stated performance criteria have been met; this is the process at the heart of National Vocational Qualifications (NVQ). Alternatively, a lecturer may assess a written assignment from a student, marking by comparing the work to an ideal model or to an agreed marking scheme.

The above processes attempt to measure the success of the training output. This does not necessarily mean that the overall objectives have been achieved; the training may have been successful, but it may not have been appropriate to meet the overall objectives. An example might be in the revised driving test procedure; the learner may well be able to reverse into a parking space, but does this make for a safer driver? Sometimes the process of checking to see if the training objectives were the right ones is also called validation. More properly this wider view of training effectiveness is called evaluation. It will usually be considering the effect of the training on groups of people or on the entire organisation. It will usually need a longer term, research type, approach.

This management report will avoid being too pedantic with these terms; what is being described should be clear from the context. Jenny Sweeny has produced some good definitions for the Industrial Society, and these are included in Appendix 1.

Evaluation can introduce other factors, notably the cost effectiveness of training. It should also consider the added value of training by comparing the after-training state with the before-training state, and the comparison with a control group who did not receive the formal training. The ability to use Windows programs on PCs would be an interesting example of this. Self learning by trial and error, and informal user groups, could well be more effective than formal teaching sessions.

Evaluation tends to be a neglected part of training. If considered at all, it is usually thought about at a late stage in the training process. Perhaps in an action oriented culture people move on to the next training experience as soon as one is completed. Perhaps people are frightened that true evaluation could cast doubts on the value of many formal training activities. Absence of at least some evaluation can lead to an enormous waste of resources. This management report will approach evaluation in a practical way, with some views on the value of different types of evaluation.

CHAPTER 2

THE TRAINING PROCESS

2.1 HOW DO YOU SEE TRAINING?

Before we introduce some basic concepts of training, you might like to ask yourself how you see training.

- Do you avoid it if possible?
- Is it only for new starters?
- Do you train in respond to demands?
- Do you train when production is slack and people would otherwise be idle?
- Do you let people choose training from a list of courses?
- Do you have training plans to meet all current job requirements?
- Do you foster individual development to meet business objectives?

Apparently positive responses to questions about training may, with further thought, not appear to be quite so positive. Recently a booklet from a national body representing UK industry quoted an example of good practice. A company was praised for arranging supervisor training at short notice to take place during a lengthy unplanned stoppage. The inference was that the training had not been planned and wasn't important enough to take supervisors away from their job under normal production conditions.

2.2 NEEDS OF LEARNERS

Most people learn by experience. The learning process is described by the Kolb learning cycle, where one has an experience, reflects on that experience, forms some ideas from the experience, tests them out and moves on to a new experience. This learning cycle needs time for reflection and testing out ideas, otherwise a series of different experiences will not lead to new learning.

Individuals will learn in different ways, usually characterised as:

- Activist, who jumps straight into action.
- Reflector, who collects data from other peoples' actions.
- Theorist, who develops theories from the data.
- Pragmatist, who uses the bits of the action that seem to work.

Well designed training will allow opportunities for different types of learners to engage with the subject. If this is not the case, poor evaluation reports from some participants

may be because there were few opportunities for them to use their preferred learning style. A group of 'activists' will respond badly to a class room lecture.

In practical terms there are limits to individual capability, often categorised in terms of stages of cognitive development. However, an apparently low limit may have been set as a result of an unsuccessful experience at school, and in later life this might be more easily overcome. Always beware of writing people off in terms of learning potential. Individual motivation to learn is probably more important than any potential limit in cognitive ability.

Preparation for learning and a positive learning environment are important for employees coming back to formal learning for perhaps the first time since leaving school.

Training should be centred on the needs of the learner and not on the needs of the training professionals or education experts.

2.3 RELATIONSHIP WITH TRAINER

The person leading a training event is often described as an instructor or trainer, more rarely as a facilitator or coach. Is the trainer there to force instruction into the participants or to help them to learn for themselves? The traditional pedagogical stance of lecturing from the front of a class has virtually disappeared from industrial training. Where training takes place in a class room setting, more enterprising methods of learning have been introduced, such as brainstorming, role plays, case studies, team exercises, etc.

In some instances the trainer or the line manager will encourage skill development during the normal course of work, by coaching and mentoring activities. Role models, where the learner models behaviour on a successful performer, may not even be aware of their contribution to the individual's development.

In the extreme, with distance learning the trainer can be quite remote from the learner. In such cases it is usually beneficial for the learner to have access to a tutor locally.

2.4 WHAT IS TO BE LEARNED?

Essential facts and information will have to be memorised. Physical skills are best learned by doing the particular task. Concepts and ideas need discussion before they are likely to be understood. Within all learning there are some core skills, generally around numeracy, literacy, problem solving skills and information technology. Learning is of

little value in itself: it needs to be applied to do tasks. If this can be done, job competence has been achieved.

An understanding of underlying principles and background knowledge will be needed in addition to basic job competence. This will allow unusual situations to be handled.

In many jobs, specific behaviours are required and these can often be developed given time.

2.5 HOW WILL TRAINING TAKE PLACE?

There are many ways of delivering training:

- Managed on-job learning.
- Off-job, but within the factory site.
- Off-site, at colleges or commercial training providers.
- During normal working hours.
- Day release and part-time courses.
- Outside working hours, by open learning or twilight training.
- Non residential or residential.
- Specially designed courses or commercially available courses.

2.6 WHO PAYS?

Most training is paid for by the employer and takes place in company time. In some cases, where the business interest in the training may be less direct, arrangements may be made where employees contribute some of their own time and/or money. This can be the case with Open University degree courses, where the employee has paid the fees and given most of the time, but the employer gives paid leave for the summer school.

Grants for training or free or subsidised training places may be available from local Training and Enterprise Councils (TEC). This is usually the best route to other government or European Commission money that may be available for training. There are some government incentives to training: notably that personal income used to pay for training to national standards is tax free.

CHAPTER 3

TRAINING NEEDS ANALYSIS

3.1 THE TRAINING PROCESS

No evaluation of training can be accomplished unless we know what we are trying to achieve. This can be at an individual, work team or organisational level. Individual and work team objectives must relate to the overall business objectives. This leads us to a logical process of identifying training needs:

1. Define the organisation's strategy.
2. Communicate the objectives required to meet this strategy to all employees.
3. Define team and individual job roles and performance standards required.
4. Identify any performance deficiency and agree training needs.
5. Agree future development plan and agree training needs.
6. Deliver training.
7. Evaluate against training needs.
8. Evaluate against the organisation's strategy.
9. Feedback to individuals.
10. Feed forward to review strategy and training needs.

3.2 CONCEPT OF TRAINING NEEDS ANALYSIS

Training needs analysis is essentially a simple procedure. Decide what is required to do the job, and assess what the individual can do now. The difference between the two is the training need. There are many proprietary methods available to formalise this procedure, often based on checklists, but on most occasions a discussion between the individual and the line manager will be sufficient. It is essential for an individual to be part of the process of agreeing a training need. Unfortunately it is not unknown for people to arrive on a training event completely in the dark as to why they are there.

Training needs can be analysed on a work team basis. Once the job requirements and standards have been defined, the team members may be given the responsibility for their individual training plans. This is on the basis that certain skills have to be present in the team at all times, but it doesn't matter which individual has the skill.

3.3 HOW WIDE IS THE SCOPE OF TRAINING?

Our training objectives must have some boundaries. As a minimum, people must be able to perform the basic job competently; however, training can go much further than that, depending on organisational strategy and individual motivation. Plotting where organisations are on the range below provides a crude measure of their investment in their people.

1 Induction training for new starters.
2 Training to meet current job requirements.
3 Flexibility training to allow a wider range of tasks to be done.
4 Training to anticipate changes in the job.
5 Training for the next post up the promotion ladder.
6 Longer term development.
7 Continuous professional development over the whole working life.
8 The learning organisation.

The question often arises in relation to longer term development as to what an organisation should support by way of training and development activities. Answers might be to provide support for training and development relevant to the individual's likely career prospects, or to take a view that any development is beneficial and exercise control through some notional annual entitlement. Organisations can vary the amount of support depending on how relevant the training is seen to be to business objectives and can expect individuals to contribute their own time if the organisation pays for activities not of immediate relevance to work. In deciding how far to go, any limits to an individual's potential must be kept in mind. Additional skills and knowledge acquisition should not be so far out of step with current work that there is really no chance to practice them in the course of normal work after training.

Learning organisations describe that ideal state where everyone is learning and at the same time helping others to learn. In this ideal state there might be no full time training staff and no clearly identifiable training budget.

3.4 WHAT IS THE REAL NEED?

Training is often seen as a universal answer to problems at work. Experience demonstrates that this is not usually true. In a famous study, the Praxis Corporation, which was devoted to improving human performance, analysed performance deficiencies at work. They found that 80% of apparent performer deficiencies arose from misunderstandings about what was expected from the job holder and a lack of accurate feedback. Skill and knowledge shortcomings accounted for 19% and mental limitations for 1% of the deficiencies. So, less than 20% of performance deficiencies could be remedied by training. This is supported by the author's experience with an

analysis of the causes of accidents on a large chemical site. Less than 5% were put down to lack of training.

Another popular misconception is that training is only about changing skills and knowledge. There are many instances where changing an individual's behaviour might be more appropriate. However, in today's business world it might be as well to remember that skilled behaviours are no substitute for basic skills and knowledge, as witnessed by life insurance and personal pensions sales people.

If little learning has taken place for a long time, possibly not since leaving full time education, there may be a need for some preparation before any formal training input. So called 'learning to learn' programmes or 'access courses' may be needed before rusty learners benefit fully from a particular training event.

Occasionally someone will have really strong desires for training and development actions which appear remote from the business need. They may be planning a career change or they may want to develop an interest outside work. Rather than say no to such requests, look for possible links to work and for arrangements where the individual contributes most of the cost of training, certainly in terms of time, and possibly in terms of part of the cost.

3.5 ORGANISATIONAL NEEDS

Organisations have training needs, both in terms of implementing current strategies and in managing changes in the internal and external environment. Most of what has been said concerning individuals can be applied to organisational training needs analysis. Since the cost of training all members of an organisation is probably going to cost more than dealing with individual training needs, it is even more important to establish the real need.

Organisational training often appears in the form of 'company initiatives', with everyone being expected to attend special off job training events. Before launching such a programme, check out the alternatives. Perhaps a programme should be tried out as a pilot in one location and results evaluated before proceeding. There may be alternatives to taking people off on a special course, such as a video and discussion pack which could be used in the course of normal work group meetings.

3.6 THINK ABOUT EVALUATION FROM THE START

If we are ever going to be able to measure the effect of training, we must be reasonably clear as to what we are trying to achieve before the training starts and the current level of competence. Agreed objectives and a measure of existing skills will be necessary for

the design of training and for its subsequent evaluation. Although this seems an obvious statement it doesn't always happen. One large organisation known to the author almost embarked on an expensive telephone answering skills programme for all its secretarial staff at the height of the 'customer care' publicity, without checking to see if it was really necessary. A series of anonymous test telephone calls quickly demonstrated that the existing skill level was more than adequate.

CHAPTER 4

ASSESSMENT AND EVALUATION PROCESSES

4.1 WHY EVALUATE?

Put simply, evaluation measures the impact of a training activity on the organisation. We can expand this simple concept of evaluation into a series of questions.

- Were the training objectives met?
- Were they the right training objectives?
- If not, what should the objectives have been?
- Were there some unexpected results (positive or negative)?
- Can improvements be made in the programme?
- Can we improve the training skills of the trainers and the learning skills of the learners?
- Can the cost effectiveness of the training be improved?
- Are there any further training needs?

In order to answer these questions we will have to design measurement techniques, collect relevant data, analyse this data, and draw conclusions. This will all take time and effort, but the reward is improved business performance and lower training costs.

4.2 WHAT TO MEASURE?

The aim is to measure improvement in skill, knowledge, competence or behaviour. It is easier to measure changes in physical skills than changes in managerial or organisational behaviour, yet large parts of the training budget are spent trying to modify these behaviours. So we must attempt measurement in all areas.

Measurement is usually thought about after the training input. In a scientific approach we should measure before and after the input, and then assess the change. If we only measure after the event, we cannot detect if the skill was actually present before training, or if the improvement was not as great as we believed. Perhaps surprisingly in a scientific age, it is extremely unusual to adopt this approach. One good application is being seen in schools with the introduction of Standard Attainment Targets and the comparison of results in standard attainment tests from one year to the next. It is hoped that this will provide a rough measure of 'added value' imparted by the school and will eliminate the effect of variations in the academic quality of the intake from school to school.

In the absence of any formal pre-training event measurement, there are two opportunities to gain a feel for the situation before the training input. Often, pre-course joining instructions are sent out. These should include training objectives and might also include some simple self assessment of current levels of skill and understanding. Alternatively, this can be done at the start of the event in an opening session. The advantage of a pre-event assessment is that it should be more objective, since doing it with the other participants leads to a cross fertilisation of views. The disadvantage is that not everyone will complete it before they arrive at the training event. Carrying out the assessment at the opening session will at least ensure that all take part.

The simplest assessment of training is to rely on the individual's own view of the effect of training input. Perhaps it is surprising how many evaluations rely on an individual's view, and in particular the end-of-course 'happy sheet'. It is easy to see the origin of this title: they always add up to at least 75% success in apparently achieving objectives, which makes trainers and participants happy. More objective forms of assessment are available.

Many assessment methods will only check out the effect you were expecting. In many cases there will be effects on participants which you may not have been expecting, and it is useful to gain some understanding of these, whether they be positive or negative. For example, an outdoor activity team building weekend should have improved team performance, but it might also have had a positive effect on internal communications and organisational culture. In an extreme case, the fact that someone had been selected to go on a particular course might make a significant effect on subsequent performance. Watch out for this effect on special courses for designated high flyers; anyone who attends may automatically enhance their self esteem and their reputation in the eyes of their colleagues. It can be difficult to identify the unexpected, but it could be worth including some open ended questions in any assessment of the course.

When designing ways of collecting evaluation data, if possible you should try to link particular parts of the input to the effect measured. Using the above example of an outdoor activity team building event, it may be that most of the benefits came from the fact that the work group were away on a residential weekend together and any training input was almost incidental. The author was involved with a small research project to investigate the value of such training to managers. It proved impossible to separate out any specific effects of the outdoor activities.

Everyone has some bias and so it is important to decide who should carry out the evaluation. Perhaps the most biased person is the individual receiving the training, yet most evaluations seem to rely solely on their views. The following people may carry out an evaluation:

- The training staff, who may be in-company or external training providers.
- The individual learners.

- The learner's line manager.
- Peer group colleagues.
- Subordinates.
- An outside observer, either from somewhere else in the organisation or from outside the organisation.

Most evaluation is done by the individual, by the trainers or by external researchers. Having said that, it is probably better if the evaluation is done by the individual's line manager or work place colleagues. After all, they are the people who will notice any real changes. The obvious route for the manager to evaluate is by a performance appraisal or personal review process, where one exists. The timing of this, often formally done once per year, may not be appropriate. Informal evaluation, with feedback to the individual, can be done at a suitable stage after training is complete. In the case of lengthy programmes, a two year part-time Master of Business Administration (MBA) for example, a good manager will carry out informal reviews as the training progresses. Evaluation by colleagues is potentially sensitive. One method is for the manager to collect results from a sample of the peer group and discuss the anonymous results with the individual.

Beware of the vested interests of trainers in carrying out evaluation of their own training courses, especially commercial training providers.

4.3 EVALUATION BY PARTICIPANTS

As has been said, this is probably the most commonly used group of evaluators. However, there are many potential pitfalls:

- Individuals are unlikely to rate their own abilities accurately. Where physical skills are involved they often exaggerate; where managerial type skills are involved they often under estimate their abilities. Many more than 50% of male drivers rate their skill as above average. Yet at the same time may underestimate their communication skills.
- Employees are unlikely to be critical of training provided by their employer.
- If a programme has an established reputation, individuals will probably hesitate to be too critical even if it has out lived its usefulness.
- Participants may not appreciate the true objectives of the training. Much of what has passed as multi-skilling training has been an attempt to change attitudes rather than to impart really essential new skills.
- Participants may not understand the measurement standard. Without any specific guidance on this, individuals will rate performance by comparison with colleagues or with their own previous performance. The idea of comparison with national standards, or with the best of the international competition, may be important.

CHAPTER 5

ASSESSMENT OF INDIVIDUAL CAPABILITIES

5.1 INTRODUCTION TO ASSESSMENT

This chapter looks at the usual results expected from a training programme, skills and knowledge, their application to carry out a job, an understanding of underlying concepts and possibly modified behaviours. There is a focus on the individual and on measuring the immediate outcomes of training.

5.2 FACTUAL KNOWLEDGE

Most jobs require some factual knowledge; an example is the London taxi driver's ability to remember all the various locations, streets and roads in the city. Indeed this is referred to as 'the knowledge' and is the subject of a rigorous test by examiners before a licence is issued.

Knowledge will only be of use if it can be applied to a real work situation. Chemical plant technicians may learn chemical engineering in a series of unit operations, reaction, distillation, separation, etc. The technicians will only be successful in complex problem solving if they can access all of this knowledge when investigating a particular problem.

Managers should be realistic in the amount of knowledge they expect individuals to know without recourse to works of reference. It will be unrealistic for new recruits to learn a three volume set of Works Instructions, but they should know the outline contents and where they can refer to the three volumes. Perhaps the only section they will have to learn in detail would be the Safety Instructions.

Remember that we shouldn't measure the training input, such as attendance on a course, we should measure the output. In the case of knowledge this is comparatively easy, although there has been some reluctance to formally measure knowledge at work. In the academic world such measures are commonplace and, where necessary, should be applied at work. Some ways of measuring knowledge are:

- Tests and examinations.
- Questioning whilst on the job.
- Off job interview.
- Pub quiz competition (this makes learning fun and potentially rewarding).

Knowledge that is essential for successful job performance will need routine re-checking, either formally or through normal supervision whilst working.

5.3 SKILLS AND APPLICATION OF SKILLS AND KNOWLEDGE

Skills vary in the degree of physical and mental ability required. Physical skills are acquired by a combination of training and practise and may require some degree of predisposition or aptitude. As technology advances it is becoming unusual for jobs to require physical skills alone. It is difficult to imagine that metal turning on a lathe originally required cutting tools to be held by hand, a rare combination of strength and accuracy. Of course, today's operation of computer controlled machining centres needs no physical skill at all but a high level of programming skills. Where physical skills are important, assessment must be by a practical demonstration:

- Apprentice test pieces.
- Drama audition.
- Evidence of previous work.
- Workplace assessment (typically the NVQ assessment process).
- A real assessment but in simulated work conditions.

In some situations this practical demonstration can include the use of so called performance aids such as check lists and aide memoires.

People may need to demonstrate that they are competent in the application of skills and knowledge before carrying out a task. This is usually achieved by testing some typical aspects rather than examining every aspect. There are many recognised qualifications based on a general demonstration of competence. In the vocational field the new National Vocational Qualifications are excellent. There are many well established professional qualifications, but exercise caution if they depend only on written examinations and length of experience. Neither will guarantee job competence.

Job skills may need regular re-checking, as with air line pilots. Usually this is achieved via normal job supervision.

Practical demonstrations of skills may be insufficient to prove competence. In most jobs there will be a need for some background knowledge and an understanding of underlying principles. While the 'trained monkey' syndrome may be sufficient to handle routine operations, more skills will be needed to cope with unexpected situations and to adapt and improve job methods. National Vocational Qualifications check this underpinning knowledge as part of the assessment process.

5.4 UNDERSTANDING OF CONCEPTS

In many jobs, skills and knowledge are not enough and the ability to understand concepts is needed. For example fault finding can require a mental image of complex interlinking systems, and an understanding of cause and effect. British Gas service engineers need an understanding of the concept of customer care as well as proficiency in servicing central heating boilers. The level of understanding of concepts can be assessed in several ways:

- Conceptual skill and mental reasoning tests.
- Questioning techniques, formal and informal.

5.5 BEHAVIOURS

Specific behaviours often distinguish the top performers rather than any particular skills or knowledge. This tends to be more so in management roles where teams need to be motivated and external groups influenced. Successful performers' behaviour can be analysed to find the key distinguishing factors. Although there is a belief that you cannot significantly change some behaviours, others can be modified or reinforced. This leads to special training and the need for assessing the changes. Assessment can be by several methods:

- Observation during the normal course of work.
- By a rating questionnaire completed by the boss, the individual and/or subordinate.
- By a structured interview which probes real events from recent work experience.

5.6 MEASUREMENT AGAINST STANDARDS

We can measure changes in performance or we can measure performance against a standard. At work, standards are generally applied to the minimum acceptable performance. In the academic world standards are used to provide a rating, GCSE grades for example, rather than a minimum acceptable standard. This has led to misunderstanding about NVQs. The fact that we expect virtually everyone to pass does not imply a lowering of standards. On the basis that people would not remain in employment if their performance was consistently below the minimum standard, it is reasonable that most people will achieve the NVQ. NVQs are not about the pursuit of excellence.

External standards must be well defined and relevant to the actual business. NVQs are now available for most business activities and their definition is subject to rigorous quality control by the National Council for Vocational Qualifications (NCVQ). There are other national and industry standards, but these will probably be replaced by NVQs.

External standards are unlikely to be an exact fit with your specific training requirements. They also need applying to your work situation. So, for example, although the Process Industry NVQ for operators will demand that safety procedures are followed at all times, it obviously cannot spell out what these procedures contain since they will vary from plant to plant. So we cannot rely solely on external standards. As there is pressure on the NCVQ to reduce the number of separate NVQs and to rationalise across 'similar' industries, more care will need to be taken over reliance on external standards alone.

In any assessment process the accuracy of assessment and the quality of the assessors will be issues. This is particularly true of the relatively new NVQ standards, where numerous organisations offer assessor training and assessments. It is easy to over-train, both in terms of what is needed to meet NVQ standards and in setting up your own internal assessment system. For example, it is difficult to believe that experienced secondary school teachers would require much additional training before they can meet the class room training standards of the Training and Development NVQ.

CHAPTER 6

APPLICATION OF ASSESSMENT TECHNIQUES

6.1 SELECTION AND INDUCTION TRAINING

The starting point for any new recruitment is a clear definition of the job and a person specification. Leaving aside selection issues, there may be some minimum entry standards which require assessment at the time of selection. Following recruitment there may be a programme of induction training. Since most employees soon forget what it is like to start a new job, evaluation of the induction programme by the new recruits is important.

6.2 TRAINING PROGRAMMES

This will be the focus of much attempted evaluation. It is worth repeating that evaluation must be considered at the start of the process as training needs are agreed and suitable training is designed. Then evaluation will include assessments before, during and after the formal training input. The assessments after training may be immediately afterwards and at three or six months down the track. In the case of major organisational training initiatives a longer time scale may be appropriate. Finally there may be occasional checks in the future to ensure that the required skills are still in place. Let us look at each stage in more detail.

Pre-course checks are useful to see if the proposed training programme is appropriate for the individual's real needs. Ask why each individual has been nominated. Acceptable reasons might be as an action from a performance review, or as preparation for a future job. Unacceptable reasons might be because the individual selected the course from a list of available courses, or because production was slack and there was time to do some training. Training staff should not be afraid to challenge line managers' nominations.

Line managers should be involved in briefing individuals prior to training. Learning objectives can be agreed and initial thought given to practice and application when returning to the normal job.

Participants can be asked for a statement of personal objectives at the start of the course. This is good since it establishes that people are on the right course (!) and gives some level of personal commitment to learning on the course. At the end of the training, individuals can check if they feel that their personal objectives have been met.

During training, tutors should continuously and informally assess individuals. Presentations by participants during the course assists with this process, as well as demonstrating successful learning to other participants.

As mentioned above, tutors should check to see if individual objectives have been met at the end of the course. At the end of some courses there will be a formal assessment of skill. If not, it can be possible to incorporate assessment in an acceptable way. Examples might be team competitions or a quiz with small prizes.

The most common form of evaluation is the use of a questionnaire hand out at the end of the course. This usually covers achievement of objectives, administration, location and facilities and teaching style. These questionnaires are good at evaluating administration, facilities and teaching. They are of doubtful value in measuring the achievement of objectives and probably useless as a means of evaluating potential changes in skills or behaviours. When used, there should be sufficient time allowed to complete the questionnaire; often they are handed out at the end of the programme so that the sooner the individual completes it the sooner they are on the road home. It is better to do it earlier in the day, and give some feedback to the group at the end of the course, possibly with a brief discussion.

Good managers will always try to follow up training with their people when they return to work. This can pick up on training objectives agreed before the course and how the learning will be put into practice. If individual difficulties have been experienced there may be a need for the manager to carry out some additional coaching to ensure maximum benefit from the course. At the very least there should be some management recognition of the training. It is very demoralising to return fired up with enthusiasm and implementation plans from a course, only to be greeted by a boss with a pile of urgent jobs asking where on earth have you been for the past week!

Valuable measurements can be made around the six month mark. Enough time will have elapsed to allow new skills to be used, yet the pre course state and the learning experience will be fresh in peoples' minds. There are several methods of collecting evaluation data at this stage; which approach is appropriate depends on the importance of the training and the resources available. Before any participants are contacted, the method of assessment must be designed and tested. It is usual to use some form of questionnaire, either to be completed and returned, or used as a guide to a structured interview. Questions should relate to the application of the training following the course. If the questionnaire is at all complex it should be tried out on a pilot basis and modified as necessary before starting the full survey. Possible means of collecting data are:

- Individual face-to-face interviews with all or with a sample of participants.
- Postal questionnaires, sent to participants, probably to immediate managers, and possibly to colleagues.
- Telephone interviews.

Any training experience should always be reviewed at the time of the next individual appraisal by the line manager.

On occasions, a follow up event might be an integral part of the training programme. This will enable participants to share experiences of how they have applied the training and what business benefits resulted. Obviously this can provide an excellent source of evaluation data.

6.3 INDIVIDUAL DEVELOPMENT

Individual development implies something beyond the immediate needs of the current job. Many organisations see this as an essential investment in the valuable asset of their employees. The starting point is an individual discussion, preferably with the line manager, leading to an agreed development plan. Some organisations take responsibility for longer term development away from line managers; one company brings local college staff into the workplace to discuss and agree longer term development plans with employees. The danger with this approach is that development is seen as somewhat irrelevant to work and that development can only take place in external courses and evening classes.

Self assessment is valuable in establishing individual development plans, either as an individual activity or in specially designed career planning workshops. Well designed in-house selection events for promotional opportunities can incorporate elements of individual development planning for the people who are not selected. This can be a powerful stimulus to individuals to start to develop their skills so as to improve their chances next time. Having said that, individual development should not be seen as only leading to promotion.

As with all development, regular reviews, both formal and informal, are vital.

A more formal assessment of work based activities, such as projects or special investigations, can help evaluate individual development progress. And one should always listen for informal feedback from colleagues.

6.4 WHEN TO EVALUATE

Since much of this aspect has already been covered, this section will focus on the longer term evaluation. Sufficient time must elapse after training to allow practice of the new skills, recycling of any learning or application problems, and for them to become assimilated into normal working. Then a true measure of the lasting effect may be obtained. It is usual to do this after three or six months, or after one or two years. If you are interviewing an individual some time after a training event, try not to lead with the

information that you are assessing the effect of that specific course. If possible, approach the evaluation by asking how well the individual feels that he or she manages the particular aspects covered in the course, without naming the course immediately. The following questions might be useful.

- What has helped them?
- What techniques are useful?
- Where did they learn about them?

6.5 USE OF INDEPENDENT EVALUATORS

Independence is an important quality in any evaluation, although in practice most evaluation will be led by the training function or by line management. It is possible to engage an external consultant to carry out an evaluation; however it should not be the one providing the training. Local schools, colleges or universities may have a research assistant or student looking for such a project.

Investors-in-People is a national standard for the investment an organisation makes in its employees. Much of this investment will be in terms of training and development. The Investors-in-People process uses independent assessors to evaluate all aspects of training and development.

Finally do not neglect your own staff. There may be an employee on an Open University course who has not been involved in the particular programme under evaluation, and who is seeking an assignment topic. Alternatively it may be worth setting up a small team of young managers to do the evaluation. In these ways you get a double benefit: the evaluation is done and some employees gain an insight into evaluation techniques.

6.6 EVALUATION DESIGN

Some examples of good evaluation design are included in Appendices 2 to 4. More information about the Investors-in-People evaluation is included in Appendix 5.

CHAPTER 7

COST EFFECTIVENESS

7.1 WHAT IS COST EFFECTIVE TRAINING?

Cost effectiveness is simply the cost of doing the training compared with the financial benefits obtained from the training. There is a potential problem in that it is much easier to measure the cost of training rather than the benefits. This can lead to senior managers and directors reducing the investment in training, especially in times of tight finances. Yet it is often this very time that it is best to invest in training so as to be ready for an up-turn. Also, we should not expect an immediate pay back on training investment. Most capital investment is justified on the basis of benefits over perhaps several years. The same attitude is rarely used with investment in people, yet it is unusual for full benefits of training to be realised immediately a course has ended. For example, benefits may only show when all of the work team have completed the training.

Occasionally the cost comparison should be with the cost of not doing the training. This might be in product quality terms, or occasionally it can be the case with major disasters, where unfortunately you do not know the cost of not doing the training until it is too late.

The costs of training are fairly easy to identify and include:

- Course fees.
- Annual budget of in house training department.
- Supervisors' time spent training staff in the work place.
- Covering job (eg overtime) while individual is being trained.
- Management time spent on developing a training strategy and then reviewing it.
- Travel and residential costs.
- In-company training premises, especially the residential training establishment out in the country.

The cost benefits realised by training can include:

- Improved productivity.
- Increased plant availability.
- Improved conformance to standards.
- Reduced costs of correcting mistakes.
- Fewer accidents.
- Better suggestions to improve products and services.
- Less need to bring in outside specialists.

The cost of not training, while including the converse of the above benefits, may be spectacularly high. This happens when disasters are due to lack of proper training. Stark examples of this were the Clapham rail disaster, where lack of proper training for technicians wiring up new signalling equipment was a significant factor, and the Piper Alpha oil rig explosion which was partly due to lack of training in safe maintenance procedures.

7.2 CONTROL OF TRAINING COSTS

Since it is difficult to measure the cost benefits, one approach to controlling costs is to minimise the expenditure needed to meet the training objectives. Some practical ways of controlling training costs are:

- Give line managers the training budget for their people.
- Rigorously question the need for in house training facilities.
- Question the extra benefit of residential training.
- Be careful with the use of external consultants, both in terms of fees and duration of their involvement with you.
- Maximise the use of subsidised local services, for example from Training and Enterprise Councils (TEC), colleges, universities, etc.
- Investigate possible collaboration with other companies (this may open the door to a TEC grant).
- Use of industry organisations, Confederation of British Industry, Institute of Directors, Industrial Society, etc., who run a wide range of training programmes.
- Investigate grants to help cover the cost of training. A booklet 'Paying for Training' is published annually by the Planning Exchange (see Additional Information section).

In addition, concentrate on developing cost effective delivery processes as an alternative to the traditional off-job course. Some ideas are:

- Use the line manager as a coach.
- Link training programmes to work by devices such as work based projects.
- Maximise the use of open learning, where learners study in their own time or in non-productive time at work.
- Managed on-job experience. This should be distinguished from the discredited 'sitting with Nellie' system, where a trainee was merely placed alongside an experienced employee in the hope that they would pick up how to do the job.
- Twilight training at the end of the work period, partly in work time and partly in leisure time.
- Job swaps or temporary secondments to a different work place or job.
- The 'buddy' system, where an expert and a learner are paired up to work together. This is especially good if the expert in one subject is a learner in the buddy's field of

expertise. The author saw this work well in cross instrument/electrical training, where an instrument supervisor was paired up with an electrical supervisor.

CHAPTER 8

EVALUATING THE EFFECT ON THE ORGANISATION

8.1 EFFECTS ON ORGANISATIONS

It is usual for training to be seen as having an effect on the individual learner and to be assessed and evaluated in this context. In many organisations the effect on the organisation will be the real desired outcome and this may be more than the effects on the individuals. For example, many companies have embarked on flexibility or multi-skilling training to allow individuals to carry out a wider range of tasks. While this skills training is undoubtedly required, the message that the organisation has demonstrated its willingness to spend money to improve work practices may be more important in delivering the desired changes.

Usually the training objectives will be met by a particular programme, but with hindsight it might be realised that these objectives were not critical in influencing the situation. In an example familiar to the author, a site-wide safety campaign was introduced to improve safety performance, particularly in terms of reduced serious accidents involving time off work. Training actions included:

- A full day's off-job safety training for all employees.
- Training for first line managers in leading safety work group discussions.
- An optional one day off-job event examining personal motivation in connection with safe working.

In addition there were other actions taken to demonstrate that safety really was top priority:

- Safety was at the top of meeting agendas.
- Production was actually stopped if there were any doubts on safety.
- Publicity and an incentive scheme were introduced to reduce lost time accidents.
- The Site Manager personally interviewed everyone who had a serious accident.
- Safety performance was seen to influence senior managers' pay and promotion prospects.

The campaign did result in a spectacular improvement in safety performance. However, it was not at all clear which of the many actions had made a significant impact. Whether this matters is, of course, debatable given the results. It is just that evaluation may have enabled other sites to adopt the effective parts of the strategy and achieve the results at reduced cost and effort.

8.2 SOME ORGANISATION WIDE MEASURES

It is possible to measure the effect of training, or the lack of it, on the organisation. Some useful measures are:

- Reductions in set-up time and downtime.
- Reductions in waste.

These are probably the only 'bottom line' measures which are directly affected by training capability. It is extremely difficult to look for the specific effect training has had on company turnover and profit, staff turnover and absence, customer satisfaction, etc. Long term trends in these parameters might be linked to training, but without extensive research it will be difficult to be certain.

Although one should beware of measuring training inputs, it can be worth looking at:

- Percentage of employees with individual training plans.
- The progress towards delivery of these plans.
- The number of NVQs and other occupational standards achieved by employees.
- Company progress towards the Investors-in-People Award.
- Percentage of employees engaged in individual development activities such as voluntary further education.

Beware of the following training input measures:

- Number of days spent on training, which might imply that the more days were spent on training, the better the job. The logical conclusion is all training and no production.
- Training budget per employee.
- Training budget as a percentage of total budget.
- Number of full time training staff or the ratio of training staff to employees.

These measures may be used in benchmarking exercises where companies compare themselves with the 'best in class' organisations. Here they can be useful in giving some indications of why training results are inferior, but should not be used as a primary comparison.

The most cost effective training is that which is undertaken continuously, as an integral part of the job, with everyone contributing to training colleagues and at the same time learning something new themselves. This ideal has become known as the learning organisation, where everyone is a trainer and everyone is a learner.

8.3 ORGANISATIONAL CLIMATE

This is a key area. If you get this right, you may not need to do any formal training at all! Organisational climate surveys will include some measure of the effect of training on the organisation. A good survey will show how individuals perceive relationships at work, which will determine how great is their discretionary contribution (how much more they are prepared to put into a job over the minimum job requirements).

Factors affecting climate include:

- Individual feeling of self worth.
- Relationships to colleagues and work team.
- Relationship to immediate boss.
- Relationship to external customers.
- Individual's relationship to the organisation as a whole.
- Effectiveness of operating systems, procedures and support services.

Questionnaires can be used to measure climate. Care should be taken in designing the questions. This point can be illustrated by the following statements relating to views of the reward system; respondents are asked for their level of agreement with the statements. They are real examples from different commercially available climate surveys.

'People who do well in the organisation tend to be those who know how to please their supervisor, and are able and willing to use power and politics to get ahead'

'Our reward system is fair'

'My supervisor rewards people in proportion to the excellence of their performance'

'People in this organisation expect to do better every year'

To the author's mind, one of these statements is too cynical, one is too idealistic and one is too specific. The moral is not to go out and purchase an evaluation system without studying its approach and style.

Questions can be designed to demonstrate the positive behaviour which will lead to an improvement in the particular area. Rather than simply ask if an individual feels free to talk to anyone at work, why not suggest when this might be done. By asking if people are co-operative when trying to achieve common goals, and willing to cross organisational boundaries in order to get the job done, the desired behaviours are suggested. Again these are real examples from surveys.

CHAPTER 9

EVALUATION BY COMPARISON WITH OTHER ORGANISATIONS

9.1 BENCHMARKING

Benchmarking is about comparing your organisation with the best performers in the field. It is usual to look for exemplars in a similar market, technology or product field to your own, but in the case of training there is no reason to put too tight a restriction on organisations examined. Look at other companies in similar operations and look at companies in completely different fields. Try to find out which companies are good at training. Possible sources of this information might be:

- Who has been awarded Investors-in-People?
- Who gives presentations at relevant conferences?
- Winners of national training awards.

Before visiting a company in connection with benchmarking, be clear about what specific activities you are collecting data about. In the case of training, you should be looking at objective measures such as the proportion of staff with NVQs, and any evaluation reports, not at the training inputs of how many days are spent on training etc. When seeking benchmarking data for training, remember some of the words of caution in the previous chapter. There may be special factors to take into account in explaining differences:

- Do they have to train people from scratch, or is there a pool of appropriately skilled people available?
- Is there a high turnover of people?
- How fast is the technology or product change?
- The other training activities include youth training schemes, apprentice training, etc. The numbers of trainees on such schemes may not be directly related to business needs.
- Are there any statutory requirements to train and retrain?
- How evenly is the training resource divided among employees? In some organisations a disproportionately high percentage of the training budget may be spent on comparatively small groups of employees, such as apprentices, graduate recruits, identified high fliers, etc.

CHAPTER 10

EVALUATION AGAINST NATIONAL STANDARDS

10.1 INVESTORS-IN-PEOPLE

Investors-in-People is a national standard designed to assess how seriously an organisation is over the training and development of its staff. Many organisations have glibly said that people are their most important asset. The Investors-in-People standard allows them to measure this and to look for improvements. As a bonus it also provides some national recognition. The standard is designed around the deceptively simple sequence of agreeing a business strategy, explaining it to all your employees, agreeing training plans with each one of them, delivering the training and reviewing. There is little point in fully describing the standard here. Full details are available from local Training and Enterprise Councils (TEC) in England and Wales or Local Enterprise Companies (LEC) in Scotland.

Investors-in-People is recommended by the author as a means of evaluating commitment to training and achievement of results. A key feature of the process is the alignment to business performance: training is not seen as an end in itself as was possibly the case in the old Training Levy days and the Industrial Training Boards. The process of understanding the standards and testing yourself against them gives the benefits, the actual award itself is almost incidental.

Some extracts from the Investors-in-People standard on evaluation are included in Appendix 5.

CHAPTER 11

DESIGN OF EVALUATION QUESTIONNAIRES

11.1 INTRODUCTION

Most methods of collecting data for the evaluation process will be based on a questionnaire. This questionnaire may be completed directly by the participant, colleague or manager, or it may be used as the basis for a telephone or face to face interview. A standard questionnaire may be used for every course, but if time allows it is better to design one specifically for individual courses. There are some general guidelines to follow when designing questionnaires, based on the following principles:

- Only collect data relevant to the evaluation.
- Design most of the collection process so that it is possible to analyse the data fairly easily. It is better to ask respondents to choose one of a set of words or phrases that is nearest to their feelings, rather than have them express something in their own words.
- Include an open ended question to capture any unexpected outcomes.
- Find out what use participants have made, or will be making, of their new skills and knowledge
- Keep the objectives in mind.
- When participants are back at work it is not realistic to expect them to devote too much time to completing a questionnaire, so keep it simple and brief.
- It is usual to leave responses anonymous, but you may need to ask about job role and length of experience in order to put responses into context.
- Give respondents the opportunity to see the results of the evaluation.

11.2 DESIGN OF QUESTIONNAIRES

The best advice is to look at some of the examples included in the Appendices to this management report and to base your questionnaire on relevant extracts and ideas. Some practical hints include:

- When using a scale of either numbers or words, avoid a mid point so that fence sitting is eliminated. Some evaluations go so far as to force respondents to choose the one of two extremes. For example 'I believe all programmes should be fully evaluated' or 'I believe all evaluations are a waste of time'.

- Avoid putting hidden values on questions. The example given above may elicit a different response if the second statement had been 'I believe that scarce training resources should concentrate on training rather than evaluation'.

- If giving a choice, ensure an even distribution about the mid point. A common scale is 'strongly agree/mildly agree/mildly disagree/strongly disagree'. If this is skewed to 'very strongly agree/strongly agree/mildly agree/disagree', obviously you are likely to gain greater agreement to your proposition. The author remembers a questionnaire by one of the leading environmental campaign groups which used skewed choices.

- Be careful about varying the layout of responses. If you suddenly reverse the implication of a 'strongly agree', or introduce a negative question in a series of positive questions, you risk getting inaccurate results. After all, in a recent parliamentary by-election 10000 people voted for a 'literal democrat' candidate. Some evaluators claim that by varying the layout of questions respondents are prevented from adopting a mechanistic approach to the questionnaire, but this is a risky strategy.

- If you ask for a numerical response, say between 1 and 6, make sure you make it clear whether you are asking for relative importance, in which case 1 is the highest, or for points scoring, in which case 1 is the lowest.

- Always thank respondents for the completed questionnaire. You may want to offer a small incentive to return them: a draw for a bottle of wine might be acceptable. If it is a postal response include a stamped addressed envelope.

11.3 USING THE DATA

Although it might seem obvious, there is no point collecting data which will not be used, or in making evaluation recommendations which will not be implemented. Consider holding a meeting of managers, participants and trainers to discuss evaluation results and to make recommendations. This will be worthwhile for larger programmes, or after a series of smaller programmes. Publish the results of evaluations. If the evaluation leads to a modification of a repeat series of programmes, tell the new participants about the changes. You may ask them to comment on their perception of the value of these changes at the end of their programme.

CHAPTER 12

SUMMARY AND EVALUATION

12.1 SUMMARY

1. Analyse training needs to produce individual and organisational training objectives.

2. Think about evaluation processes at the training design stage.

3. Try to measure the state prior to training so as to be able to measure the effect of training.

4. Think about who best to carry out evaluations.

5. There are differences in the ways of assessing knowledge, skills, job competence, the understanding of concepts and behaviours.

6. Measurement and evaluation should take place before, during and after a training input. A full evaluation can only be attempted some long time after the training.

7. The cost of training is best controlled by questioning the need for training and by concentrating on cost effective delivery methods.

8. Benchmarking training activities are useful but beware of using spurious parameters for the comparison.

9. Investors-in-People provides an excellent national standard against which to evaluate training and development activities.

Remember that any evaluation you attempt is likely to be better than no evaluation, so long as you implement the resulting lessons. The simplest form of evaluation is to talk to a few participants about the training and how it has helped back in the work place.

12.2 EVALUATION OF THIS REPORT

The publishers commissioned this report from the author in order to provide practical information - which is easy to digest - on measuring the effectiveness of training. It seems only fair to include a form of evaluation which could be used to assess its effectiveness at meeting this objective. Since these issues are both subjective, it would be sufficient to ask two questions:

- 'Do you consider the report practical?'
- 'Was it easy to digest?'

We could ask for a yes/no response, but presenting a range of possible answers is better.

We might wish to take advantage of the response to collect more data, but this should not be overdone. We should also have a purpose in collecting data, possibly thinking in terms of how to improve the report if it were to be updated. We could ask what were the most and least useful parts of the report, but bearing in mind the likely wide range of readers in terms of experience, prior experience and current responsibilities this would probably generate a wide range of responses. It would be better to ask if there were any missing topics or areas where readers wanted more information.

It is tempting to ask what use readers have been able to make of the information and ideas in the report. Before doing this we would need to have some means of classifying this data, otherwise the responses would be unmanageable.

The evaluation form included here can be photocopied and returned to the author if you wish. I will use responses to help improve the text if a second edition is contemplated.

12.3 EVALUATION QUESTIONNAIRE FOR THE REPORT

Report under evaluation: The assessment and evaluation of training: a practical guide.

Purpose of evaluation: To suggest improvements to the report.
To investigate potential demand for related reports.

Although your response can be anonymous, it would help to evaluate the responses if you could give the following details about yourself. Please circle the description which most nearly describes your situation.

Current position: practising trainer / training manager / personnel / line manager / director or chief executive / other (specify)

Type of business: manufacturing / service / education / other (specify)

Your training experience: over five years / one to five years / less than one year/ training is not a significant part of my role

Now please comment on the report. Do this by circling the appropriate phrase.

Practical use to you? a great deal / a reasonable amount / a little / none at all

Easy to understand? very easy / quite easy / quite difficult / very difficult

If you found it difficult to understand, please briefly explain why this was.

Please say if any aspect was missing or not adequately covered in order to meet your needs.

Are there any other topics on which you would like similar reports?

Thank you very much for completing this questionnaire. Please post the completed questionnaire to:

Dr Ian Pearce
Durham University Business School
Mill Hill Lane
Durham, DH1 3LB
United Kingdom

or fax to 0191 374 4748 (international fax +44 191 374 4748)

APPENDICES

The appendices have been chosen to illustrate good practice in the evaluation of training. The layout of the various documents and questionnaires has been modified to match the style of the rest of this management report, but the content has not been altered. The author would like to thank the various organisations for permission to reproduce their material.

APPENDIX 1

INDUSTRIAL SOCIETY DEFINITIONS

These definitions have been suggested by Jenny Sweeney, who until recently designed training evaluation courses for the Industrial Society.

Evaluation

A system of judging the benefits of a training activity to the participants and to their organisation.

Validation

A system of establishing whether a training activity was carried out in accordance with the objectives set for it. It does not involve whether the activity produced an ultimate benefit for those concerned.

Assessment

A system of determining whether a training activity is of an appropriate standard to count towards a formal qualification.

All of these can be applied to a single training event; for example, a modular programme designed to develop managers:

Evaluation:	Has the activity produced benefits for the participants and their organisation?
Validation:	Did the activity cover what it set out to cover? Did it use appropriate training methods?
Assessment:	Will the activity contribute to a qualification? (for example a professional institute's membership)

APPENDIX 2

PRE-COURSE INSTRUCTIONS AND EVALUATION

Appendix 2.1 Learning objectives

The first example is from a large pharmaceutical company. It specifically asks the participant to review the training with the immediate manager before and after the training event.

Appendix 2.2 Applicability assessment

The second example is from Imperial Chemical Industries PLC. It is a brief check list intended to restrict nominations for a particular course to people with responsibility for a reasonable number of subordinates. There was a problem with a successful course for line managers; every one wanted to go on it regardless of whether their job gave them the opportunity to put the training into practice. The check list should filter out unsuitable nominees.

APPENDIX 2.1 LEARNING OBJECTIVES

This is a simple example of a Learning Objectives statement which is sent to the participant prior to the event. If it is sent out with many pages of joining instructions, it is likely that a significant number of participants will not read the paper, let alone discuss it with their manager. It may be better to send an additional copy of the paper to the manager, with a request that the learning objectives are discussed before the course.

LEARNING OBJECTIVES
Before the training event spend time with your manager discussing and agreeing what you hope to be able to do at the end of the training process. Be specific, indicating personal objectives for your particular job. Record these objectives below. You may be asked to share some of these when you attend the training programme.
1.
2.
3.
4.

APPENDIX 2.2 APPLICABILITY ASSESSMENT

The 'Managing for Performance' event proved to be an extremely popular component of the ICI managers' core training programme. It was heavily over-subscribed and managers who had no opportunity to put the learning to use in their current jobs were being nominated for the event. The applicability assessment below was designed to filter out unsuitable nominations.

PART ONE

- Are you more than 25 years of age?
- Do you have more than two years ICI service?
- Are you likely to remain in this job for a minimum of six months after this event?
- Will you have been in your current role more than four months at time of this event?

If the answer to all of these questions is YES, please complete the Part Two below and attach a copy to your nomination form. If the answer to any of these questions is NO, then the event is unlikely to meet your needs at this stage. You should discuss with your line manager and training manager a plan to attend the event at a more suitable time.

PART TWO

CRITERIA	ASSESSMENT			
1. Number of people directly managed.	10+ **10 pts**	6-9 **8 pts**	2-5 **6 pts**	0-1 **2 pts**
2. Level of staff managed.	middle **4 pts**	junior **3 pts**	operators **2 pts**	none **nil**
3. Fixed costs responsibility.	>£0.5 m **10 pts**	<£0.5 m **8 pts**	<£0.1 m **6 pts**	<£.02 m **2 pts**
4. Cross-functional and inter-business demands of the job.	extensive links in and out of firm **10 pts**	cross-function links are essential **8 pts**	some link with other functions **6 pts**	work only in own function **2 pts**

5. Challenges that face you in your present role. • Developing your team • Saving costs • Reducing numbers • Re-organisation • Changed working practices • Major innovations/New business • Reducing markets • Divestment/Rationalisation	higher degree of difficulty higher payback **10 pts**	higher degree of difficulty lower payback **8 pts**	lower degree of difficulty higher payback **6 pts**	lower degree of difficulty lower payback **2 pts**

TOTAL POINTS

ASSESSMENT		
less than 21	21-26	over 26
Not applicable at this time.	May be applicable. Discuss with line manager and training manager.	Applicable.

The use of this approach was very successful in restricting nominations to managers who would find the programme of immediate use. While this obviously increased the cost effectiveness of the training, it also improved the quality of the events. Participants with relevant current challenges were able to contribute to the event, and to learn from each other.

Note that the assessment does not rule out participation for all time, it only suggests that the present time is not suitable and that the individual should plan when participation might be more appropriate.

APPENDIX 3

END OF COURSE EVALUATIONS

Appendix 3.1 Quick end of course evaluation

This is a simple questionnaire to be used at the end of a course to collect instant feedback. A novel feature is the choice of five words to describe the course, although this light hearted approach may encourage a flippant response from some participants.

Appendix 3.2 Community Transport Training evaluation

This evaluation form is more comprehensive, and probably represents the most one can reasonably expect participants to complete in their own time at the end of a course. It is used by the Community Transport Association, which represents the interests of local government and voluntary group providers of community transport. As part of their service to members they offer a comprehensive training programme. It is interesting to compare this example from a 'socially aware' training organisation with the examples from the business and academic worlds.

Appendix 3.3 Comprehensive monitoring and evaluation

This questionnaire is very detailed, and collects data on the programme content, the delivery and style of teaching and on the course environment. With such a lengthy questionnaire, time must be built into the closing stages of a training course for its completion.

Appendix 3.4 Learning log and learning application

This style of form is widely used to encourage individuals to record key learning and to think about the application of the learning back in the workplace.

Appendix 3.5 Feedback of evaluation

Finally, an extract from the report of a joint Department of Employment and Confederation of British Industry Conference shows how the results of an evaluation can be communicated to the participants.

APPENDIX 3.1 QUICK END OF COURSE EVALUATION

COURSE REACTIONNAIRE

We are constantly trying to develop and modify our courses, with a view to making them reflect the training needs of our customers. We welcome your comments on the course you have just undertaken, and would ask you to complete this questionnaire before you leave or send it back to us as soon as possible after the course.

Course Title: Date:

What I found most useful from the course:

What I found least useful from the course:

What would improve the course:

If a colleague asked me for an honest opinion about the course I would say:

Circle five words which best describe the course for you:

well tutored	interesting	helpful	interactive	exhausting
refreshing	professional	motivating	participative	exciting
insightful	challenging	hard work	irrelevant	practical
well presented	boring	basic	too long	valuable
rushed	intellectual	better than work	fun	thorough
good handouts	changed my life	disorganised	waste of time	indifferent
	nothing new		stimulating	
....		....		....

Feel free to add your own words.

APPENDIX 3.2 COMMUNITY TRANSPORT TRAINING EVALUATION

EVALUATION FORM

In order that training provided by CTA can be monitored, problems rectified and improvements made, we would be grateful if you would take a few minutes to fill in this form.

Title of Session:

Date of Session: Unit Number:

Please answer the questions on this form by circling the number which best represents your view.

4 Agree strongly **3** Agree **2** Disagree **1** Disagree strongly

CONTENT

	The content of the session:				
1	was relevant to the topic	4	3	2	1
2	met the training objectives	4	3	2	1
3	will be of practical use to me	4	3	2	1

TRAINERS AND FACILITATORS

	The trainer:				
4	gave a well organised presentation	4	3	2	1
5	showed a thorough knowledge of the subject	4	3	2	1
6	spoke clearly and to the point	4	3	2	1
7	made effective use of audio-visual materials	4	3	2	1

EQUAL OPPORTUNITIES MONITORING

	The trainer:				
8	showed awareness of people with different experiences and backgrounds, eg people with differing abilities, needs of women, etc.	4	3	2	1
9	actively ensured that everyone who wanted to contribute was able to do so	4	3	2	1
10	made sure that people had understood the points being made	4	3	2	1

GENERAL

11 Were you given useful handouts? Yes No

12 Please list some of the things you learned in this unit.

13 Please list anything you hoped to learn, but was not included in this unit.

14 Please use this space to make comments on any aspect of the session (content, venue, etc).

15 Please show your overall opinion of the unit by circling one of the following:

POOR	FAIR	GOOD	VERY GOOD	EXCELLENT

Thank you for taking the time to give us your views and completing the form.
Please return it to your facilitator or leave it in the box at the registration desk.

APPENDIX 3.3 COMPREHENSIVE MONITORING AND EVALUATION

This comprehensive set of monitoring and evaluation sheets was designed by a group of trainers as part of a workshop at the Durham University Business School. It would need to be used with an appropriate cover sheet for recording details of the course, trainer and location.

DELIVERY AND STYLE

6 = Excellent	3 = Fairly poor
5 = Good	2 = Poor
4 = Fairly good	1 = Very poor

Comments on specific aspects
(please asterisk those which are particularly important)

		Favourable	Unfavourable
Tutor experience/knowledge	6 5 4 3 2 1		
Tutor flexibility	6 5 4 3 2 1		
Tutor motivation/enthusiasm	6 5 4 3 2 1		
Teaching skills	6 5 4 3 2 1		
Use of technology	6 5 4 3 2 1		
Use of handout/visual aids	6 5 4 3 2 1		
Use of case study	6 5 4 3 2 1		
Opportunity for participation	6 5 4 3 2 1		
Opportunity for practice	6 5 4 3 2 1		
Tutor rapport with group	6 5 4 3 2 1		
Pace of programme	6 5 4 3 2 1		

Suggestions for improvement:

COURSE ENVIRONMENT

6 = Excellent	3 = Fairly poor
5 = Good	2 = Poor
4 = Fairly good	1 = Very poor

		Comments on specific aspects (please asterisk those which are particularly important) Favourable	Unfavourable
The venue	6 5 4 3 2 1		
Teaching room(s)	6 5 4 3 2 1		
Relaxation area	6 5 4 3 2 1		
Meals/refreshments	6 5 4 3 2 1		
Staff courtesy/helpfulness	6 5 4 3 2 1		
Course administration	6 5 4 3 2 1		
Teaching equipment	6 5 4 3 2 1		
Handouts/visual aids	6 5 4 3 2 1		

Suggestions for improvement:

PROGRAMME

6 = Excellent	3 = Fairly poor
5 = Good	2 = Poor
4 = Fairly good	1 = Very poor

		Comments on specific aspects (please asterisk those which are particularly important) Favourable	Unfavourable
Joining instructions	6 5 4 3 2 1		
Pre-course work	6 5 4 3 2 1		
Size of group	6 5 4 3 2 1		
Balance of group	6 5 4 3 2 1		
Delegate suitability (ie at the right level for coming on the course)	6 5 4 3 2 1		
Coverage of content	6 5 4 3 2 1		
Achievement of course objectives	6 5 4 3 2 1		
Delegates feedback (discussion on evaluations)	6 5 4 3 2 1		

Suggestions for improvement:

APPENDIX 3.4 LEARNING LOG AND LEARNING APPLICATION

These examples are based on handouts used by a large pharmaceutical company, but there are many variations on a similar style. They are retained by the participants.

LEARNING LOG

During the training programme there will be useful ideas or key learning points you will want to apply in the work place.

KEY IDEAS / LEARNING POINTS	HOW I WILL APPLY THESE BACK AT WORK

LEARNING APPLICATION

After the training event spend time with your manager discussing and agreeing how you can transfer the learning at work

Try to identify opportunities for applying the new skills and record these below.

ACTION PLANNED (AND DATES)	REVIEW AND COMMENTS

APPENDIX 3.5 FEEDBACK OF EVALUATION

Participants will usually be curious about the comments written on evaluation questionnaires. If there is the opportunity to give some feedback it will not only satisfy this curiosity, but will encourage the individual to complete future evaluations with the knowledge that the organisers are listening to the responses. This example is from an appendix to the published report of a conference organised by the Employment Department and the Confederation of British Industry. The event was titled 'Individuals and Learning Conference' and was held on 27 June 1994.

EVALUATION OF CONFERENCE

ATTENDANCE AND ORGANISATION

1 196 people attended the conference, with 52 returning their evaluation forms. This represented a response rate of 26%.

2 Of those completing their evaluation forms, nearly 70% said that the conference programme was good, with a further 23% saying that it was acceptable. 92% said that the organisation of the event was good, with 96% saying that the venue was good or excellent.

COMMENTS

3 On the basis of these responses, it is fair to say that the conference was extremely well received and specific criticisms should be seen in this light. Specific criticisms cited by those returning their questionnaire included the following:

- The careers service should have been invited to participate on the panel of experts.
- More employers and trade union representatives should have been invited.
- It was difficult to tell whether the conference was about young people or adults, or the learning needs of the employed or the unemployed.
- The keynote speeches could have been delivered in a more upbeat fashion.
- Some of the groups were telling shops rather than creative workshops.
- There was little new apart from the TEC National Council report.

LESSONS FOR THE FUTURE

4 For the future, some delegates thought that there should be fewer keynote speeches, leaving more time for discussion, and information packs should be sent out in advance.

APPENDIX 4

LONGER TERM EVALUATION

Appendix 4.1 Evaluation by colleagues

Pilat UK Limited* is a consultancy with considerable experience of evaluating training and development programmes. They have designed comprehensive evaluation processes for the development programmes for a number of organisations together with supporting software. The evaluation of the Executive Development Programme of a large UK pharmaceutical company involved the collection of data from a variety of sources. The example reproduced here is a questionnaire sent out to the colleagues of a course participant; a more extensive questionnaire is sent to the participant.

Appendix 4.2 Telephone survey

Appendix 4.3 Long term evaluation

The fairly long evaluation of the Durham University Business School Graduate Associate Programme (GAP) is reproduced here. Even in such a comprehensive evaluation it is difficult to find evidence for achievement of the primary objective. This is to improve the economy of the North East of England by helping small businesses employ more graduates.

* Pilat UK Limited, 29 Hendon Lane, Finchley, London N3 1PZ

APPENDIX 4.1 EVALUATION BY COLLEAGUES

EVALUATION OF EXECUTIVE DEVELOPMENT PROGRAMME

(Questionnaire for colleagues)

Q1 Please assess the extent to which there have been observable improvements in the way your colleague has been doing his/her job since he/she returned from the programme:

1 No improvement
2 A little improvement
3 Significant improvement
4 Major improvement

Q2 In general, to what extent has your business unit benefited from an even more positive contribution from your colleague since he/she returned from the programme:

1 Not at all
2 A little
3 Significantly
4 Very much

Q3 Please give examples of the way in which new knowledge and skills, that your colleague has gained in the programme, may have translated into tangible results, eg new business initiatives, organisational changes, technical revisions. Also, please indicate any financial gains that may have been achieved, or expected in the coming two to three years.

Q4 Please indicate the extent to which your colleague has displayed the following changes in behaviour and approach since he/she returned from the programme.

1 Not at all 2 A little 3 Significantly 4 Very much 5 Already a key strength*

More strategic	1	2	3	4	5
Taking more account of wider picture	1	2	3	4	5

* If you believe that no change has taken place and the individual already has a key strength, circle 5.

More aware of the competition	1	2	3	4	5
Being more customer/market driven	1	2	3	4	5
Finding better ways to overcome blockages	1	2	3	4	5
Collaborating more with other functions	1	2	3	4	5
Managing change more effectively	1	2	3	4	5
Collaborating more internationally	1	2	3	4	5
Minimising unnecessary internal competitiveness	1	2	3	4	5
More results oriented	1	2	3	4	5
More demanding of performance	1	2	3	4	5
Taking more accountability	1	2	3	4	5
Using resources more efficiently	1	2	3	4	5
Making more and better use of financial information	1	2	3	4	5
Generating more effective teamwork	1	2	3	4	5
Listening and communicating more	1	2	3	4	5
Providing clearer direction to his/her subordinates	1	2	3	4	5
Empowering his/her subordinates	1	2	3	4	5
Generating more enthusiasm	1	2	3	4	5
Creating more and better ideas	1	2	3	4	5
More open minded	1	2	3	4	5
More challenging	1	2	3	4	5
Taking more risks	1	2	3	4	5

Q5 If you observed changes in your colleague's behaviour and attitude, which are not reflected in the above list, please indicate them below.

Q6 Please give examples of the way in which the three top improvements from the above list have manifested themselves at work.

Q7 (Only to be completed by participant's sponsor, line manager, or director)
To what extent have your expectations been met from your participant's attendance on the programme?

1 Not at all 2 A little 3 Met expectation 4 Exceeded expectation

Please comment:

Q8 Please indicate how you relate to your colleague organisationally.

1 Line manager/director
2 Sponsor
3 Colleague. Indicate if international, functional, or local
4 Direct report

All replies will be treated in confidence and no individual data will be revealed.

Thank you for your co-operation.

Please return this questionnaire to:

APPENDIX 4.2 TELEPHONE SURVEY

TELEPHONE INTERVIEW

Course: Date of course:
Caller: Delegate/Manager:
Date of telephone interview:

Q1 What were your learning objectives in attending this training programme?

Q2 What were the most important things you learned?
(What was the most helpful? What was new? What was unexpected?)

Q3 What do you do differently as a result of this training programme?
(Have you had the opportunity to put the learning into practice? Any examples?)

Q4 Did you discuss the training programme with your manager before attending?
(If not, why not? If so, how helpful was this, and why?)

Q5 Have you discussed this programme with your manager since attending?
(How helpful was this? Have you agreed an action plan?)

Q6 Any comments about the programme itself?
(Comments may be about length, workload, content, handouts, tutors, level of participation, facilities, accommodation. Interviewers should add any specific questions here which participants may wish to ask)

Q7 Did the programme meet your needs?
(If not, who might it be suitable for?)

APPENDIX 4.3 LONG TERM EVALUATION

A QUANTITATIVE EVALUATION OF THE DURHAM UNIVERSITY 'GRADUATE ASSOCIATE PROGRAMME'

INTRODUCTION

The Durham University Business School 'Graduate Associate Programme' (GAP) programme is designed to help small businesses by encouraging them to take on graduates as employees. During the first year of employment the company is paid a subsidy towards the cost of the graduate, the graduate undergoes training for a Diploma in Enterprise Management, and both receive support and advice from the Business School as required.

The GAP programme has three main objectives, in order of importance:

1. To assist small businesses to employ, and make good use of, more graduates.
2. To encourage more graduates to work in small businesses.
3. To retain more good quality graduates in the North East of England.

The evaluation report reproduced here is adapted from a paper presented to the 1992 UKEMRA Conference by Richard Hanage of Durham University Business School. It shows that each of the objectives is being achieved and it also identifies factors that predict success. Since the report was written the difference between 'universities' and 'polytechnics' has disappeared.

THE EVALUATION OF GAP

A systematic framework for programme evaluation has been developed and has been applied to GAP, showing that the programme has been very successful. It is equally applicable to any intervention in the small and medium enterprise (SME) sector so long as the overall purpose can be defined, and measurable success criteria can be devised. The evaluation also provides objective data which can be used to improve the intervention process. In the case of GAP a number of useful correlations were found between the company data, the graduate data, and the success rates against the three main success criteria.

Having a clear understanding of how and why an intervention is successful provides a firm basis for developing new variations on the theme. Now that the basic version of GAP is well understood we are in a position to move onto more risky, but potentially even more valuable, variants such as family businesses and very small businesses.

In a logical and systematic world the evaluation steps would be mapped out before embarking on any intervention and the data-gathering would be carefully planned. However, in the real world many interventions spring from much more creative and unsystematic processes. The importance of the 'evaluation framework' is that it can be used retrospectively, if necessary, to research the effectiveness of an intervention prior to advocating it to policy-makers and disseminating it to other institutions. This has been the case with GAP. The main weakness with this approach is that the necessary data may be hard to obtain retrospectively and, in some cases, the logic of the original thinking may prove to be flawed. For this reason it is much better to plan the evaluation at the time of design of the intervention.

The policy implications are at two levels: the general and the particular. As a general rule policy-makers should insist that policy proposals which are based on existing mature interventions should include a systematic evaluation process to underpin the rhetoric. In the particular case of GAP the evaluation has shown that it is successful in achieving its aim: to improve the economy of the regions by helping SMEs to be successful. It should now be disseminated more widely in the UK and Europe.

PART 1. THE EVALUATION FRAMEWORK

The evaluation framework is a set of logically connected statements that link the overall policy objective to specific and measurable actions. In this way the degree to which the original objective has been met can be determined.

All SME interventions must have an overall high level purpose or objective which is the starting point for evaluation. This is the primary objective. In the case of GAP it is to improve the economy of the North East of England. A cascade of sub-objectives can be derived from the primary objective by asking the question 'how?' until a sub-objective has been reached which represents the specific purpose of the particular intervention. For GAP the cascade is as follows.

Primary Objective: To improve the economy of North East of England
How? - By helping existing SMEs to be successful. How? - By helping them improve their management teams. How? - By helping them to make good use of graduates

An important feature of the cascade of objectives is that each step must be supported by objective evidence, otherwise the evaluation process is invalid. This paper assumes that there is adequate evidence that the first step is valid; that helping SMEs to be successful is good for the regional economy. The further steps in the cascade are intuitively correct, but cannot be taken as 'givens'.

The evaluation process needs to provide objective evidence that better use of graduates does improve the management teams of SMEs, and that this in turn helps them to be successful.

The final step in producing an evaluation framework is to define a set of actionable objectives which are sufficient to achieve the lowest level sub-objective. These form the basis for the detailed design of the intervention. For GAP there are 4 main actionable objectives.

1. Persuade owner-managers of North East SMEs to recruit a recent graduate into a new type of job, and assist them in the process.

2. Train the graduates in skills that are useful to their SME.

3. Assist the owner-managers to make good use of their graduates and to retain them for long enough to be beneficial to the business.

4. Encourage the graduates to stay in the North East, and in the SME sector, even if they leave their initial GAP employer.

The essential feature of the actionable objectives is that they can be backed up by specific and measurable success criteria. The evaluation is complete when the following have been established:

1. Each step in the cascade of secondary objectives is proved by objective evidence either from the current evaluation or from previous research.
2. The success criteria of the actionable objectives have been measured.

Part 2 shows the measures that were chosen for the GAP actionable objectives and displays the evaluation data.

PART 2. APPLICATION OF EVALUATION FRAMEWORK TO GAP

Research shows that the programme has been highly successful against three specific criteria, six months after the end of the programme.

- Did the graduates do a good job for the GAP employer?	70%
- Did they stay in the North East?	79%
- Did they stay in the SME sector?	65%

The Durham University Business School (DUBS) introduced the Graduate Associate Programme in 1988. It is a twelve month programme in which recent graduates are introduced into small and medium enterprises in the North East as employees and receive management, business and personal development training relevant to their roles in the businesses. The programme operates as follows:

1. DUBS seek sponsors (Local Authorities, Training and Enterprise Councils, etc.) who will fund the GAP graduates on the programme. They also seek final year students, who must be from homes or colleges in the North East, and interview a selection of them for a 'long list' of candidates. From this, each business is sent a 'short list' of candidates whose skills and personal qualities match the needs of the business and the owner-manager.

2. Employment starts in September and DUBS provides a total of about 36 days training, spread throughout the year. The graduates do three work-related projects and a case study, in addition to their course work, and sit an examination at the end of the year. If successful they qualify for the Diploma in Enterprise Management.

3. The businesses pay the graduates the normal small company graduate rates (about £10000 in 1992) and receive a subsidy of £3500. They release them for the 20 days of training that occurs on weekdays, and help them find suitable projects in the company. In other respects the graduates are normal employees.

4. Although there is a moral obligation to keep the graduates on for the full twelve months of the GAP programme, the businesses can terminate their employment earlier. There is no obligation to keep them beyond the twelve months; whether they stay on is a matter of agreement between employer and employee.

Results - Success criteria

Success criteria were devised for each of the actionable objectives. These are shown below in italics, along with the evaluation data.

Actionable objective 1: Persuade owner-managers of North East SMEs to recruit a recent graduate into a new type of job and assist them in the process.

1.1 Size of businesses taking part in GAP:

100-250 staff	25%
50-99 staff	26%
20-49 staff	30%
Less than 20 staff	19%

1.2 The number of graduates employed each year:

GAP1	1988/89	17 students
GAP2	1989/90	15 students
GAP3	1990/91	11 students

Note that the decline in numbers was reversed in GAP4 (15) and GAP5 (17). The constraint on numbers was due to the reluctance of owner-managers to take on graduates. Sponsorship was available for many more students, and there were large numbers of applicants. The improvement for GAP5 was due in part to having the success data available from this evaluation.

1.3 Number of graduates carrying out new types of jobs:
It is a requirement of the programme that they are in new types of jobs, normally also in businesses that have never recruited a recent graduate before. In practice a few exceptions have been made, probably about 10% of cases.

Based on these measures of success, the first actionable objective was achieved.

Actionable objective 2. Train the graduates in skills that are useful to their SME.

2.1 Feedback from owner-managers and graduates on course content:
No quantitative data is available on feedback, but anecdotal evidence is strong. The programme has been refined as a result of the feedback including:

- Ensuring that the business studies content is aimed at SMEs and not large companies.
- Altering the Diploma to be based more on work-related projects.
- Increasing the personal development content in response to the personal relationships issues that frequently occur.

2.2 Pass rate for the Diploma in Enterprise management:

Passed first time:	38 students
Passed on re-take:	4 students
Failed to re-take	1 student

Based on this data we believe that the course content is now correct, and that the students are being successfully trained in skills directly relevant to their SMEs.

Actionable objective 3. Assist the owner-managers to make good use of the graduates and to retain them for long enough to be beneficial to the business.

3.1 Number of graduates rated by owner-manager as making a 'major contribution':
This data was collected from owner-managers.

Major contribution	70%
Paid their way	24%

Not successful 6%

Note that in at least one case the lack of success can probably be ascribed to the owner-manager rather than the graduate!

3.2 Number offered ongoing employment after the initial twelve months:

Offered ongoing employment: 65%

This is a very significant result as the salary subsidy ceases after twelve months, and owner-managers are not noted for their readiness to pay for staff who do not earn their keep. In some cases significantly better salaries and conditions were offered as inducements to stay.

3.3 Retention rates six months after the end of the GAP programme:

Stayed more than six months 42%

Stayed more than eighteen months 33%

These three success criteria combined indicate that the owner-managers achieve significant benefits from the graduates and do succeed in retaining many of them.

Actionable objective 4. Encourage the graduates to stay in the North East and in the SME sector, even if they leave their initial employer.

4.1 *Numbers of graduates staying in North East:*

	six months after GAP	eighteen months after GAP
In North East	65%	59%
In North	82%	75%
Elsewhere	18%	25%

4.2 *Numbers of graduates staying in SME sector:*

	6 months after GAP	18 months after GAP
In SMEs	79%	72%

Both of these results represent excellent retention rates. The high proportion staying in SMEs is particularly gratifying. Conversely it is good to see that the graduates can move out of the SME sector if they wish; it is important that GAP does not prevent the graduates joining bigger companies later in their careers.

Results - Cascade of sub-objectives

As mentioned earlier, more evidence is needed to confirm the validity of the links between the success of the businesses and the improvements to the management teams through more use of graduates. A very pragmatic view is that the owner-managers

would be the best judges of this and would offer the graduates employment at the end of the GAP if this was the case. The evidence was clear. As displayed above, 65% of the owner-managers offered their GAP graduates on-going employment after the programme was complete. In addition some of those that didn't make such an offer were adamant that the graduates made a 'major contribution' and that there were other factors that prevented them continuing the employment.

Is there any explanation for the offers of employment other than the hypothesis that the graduates contributed directly to the success of the businesses? None of the possibilities listed below seem likely in the cash-flow oriented world of the SME:

1. The owner-managers were sorry for the graduates.
2. They wanted to show that GAP was successful.
3. They felt it churlish to the sponsors to terminate the graduates.
4. They were philanthropists in disguise.
5. They had committed time and effort to the graduates and hoped that benefits would eventually arise.

The last of these, plus some elements of the others, could account for some of the effect or at least for a decent period between the end of GAP and the graduate leaving the SME. It is for that reason that the measures of outcomes were based on data taken six months after the end of GAP. On that basis 42% of the graduates were still with their GAP employer after they had completed eighteen months total employment.

This data fully justifies the validity of the cascade of sub-objectives.

Conclusion - Evaluation of GAP

The evaluation of GAP described above confirms that the programme meets its objectives and fully justifies the decision to disseminate it more widely to policy-makers and other providers. A final stage in evaluation would be to try to carry out a cost-benefit analysis. This is not easy. The costs are easily available, but the benefits are difficult to quantify in cash terms. An approximate analysis has been carried out, but it is not rigorous enough to include in this paper.

A further step in evaluation would be to determine which parts of the programme contribute most to its success. There are four main elements; the recruitment process, the subsidy, the Diploma training, and the business support. Each one is expensive and the cost of the programme is an issue that may constrain its dissemination. Anecdotal evidence suggests that all four are important, but more research is required.

PART 3. SELECTION OF BUSINESSES AND GRADUATES

The data about the students and the SMEs was statistically analysed for correlations with the four main quantitative success criteria; staying on with the GAP employer, making a major contribution, staying in the North East, and staying in the SME sector.

Methodology

The methodology was determined by the requirement to improve the graduate recruitment and company selection processes. Information about the graduates was extracted from their Standard Application Forms and data about the companies was based on easily available statistics. Correlations of the outcome data with the information about the graduates and the companies was examined to seek indicators of success that could be used at recruitment time. The statistical significance of all results was calculated as the student numbers (43) were relatively small and could lead to wrong conclusions being made.

Results

A number of factors have been found which can be used to predict successful graduates and businesses. If applied to the GAP applicants they would, for instance, have probably increased the rate of staying on with the GAP business from 42% to 56%. Note that the significance levels of some of the results is relatively low, so more work needs to be done with data from future GAP programmes to verify the results.

1. Factors that predict 'STAYED ON AT LEAST 6 MONTHS AFTER GAP'

The students that stay on:

	Significance
1. Are employed by the bigger businesses	>98%
2. Have medium or high A-levels results	>90%
3. Do not have high leadership indicators	>90%
4. Have engineering/science/IT. degree	>90%

This analysis confirms the observations that GAP students have more problems in the smaller businesses, and that engineers and scientists are more likely to settle well.

The effect of leadership indicators may be initially surprising, but can be rationalised on the basis that these students quickly run out of challenge in an SME, or become a threat to the owner-manager. This has been observed in several cases. Of the ten students with high leadership indicators, nine left their GAP employer quickly (and six of these also left the region).

2. Factors That Predict: 'MADE A MAJOR CONTRIBUTION'

Not surprisingly some of the factors that predict a good contribution are the same as those that predict STAYING ON. Students whose work in the GAP SME has been judged a major success:

	Significance
1. Are employed by the bigger companies	>98%
2. Do not have high leadership indicators	>98%

Note that although low A-level grades correlated highly with leaving the SME quickly, they are not correlated with a poor contribution. This seems paradoxical. Why did so many low A-level students leave if their work was going well? Although more engineers stay with the SMEs, only a few of those that left quickly were judged a success, so overall their 'major contribution' is no better than Arts/Business graduates.

3. Factors That Predict 'STAYED IN SME SECTOR'

Those that stay in the SME sector:

	Significance
1. Come from the Polytechnics	>90%

This is the only significant factor. Of the twelve GAP students from Polytechnics, eight left their GAP company quickly, and only one moved into a large company. Of the 30 University GAP students, 17 left quickly and 9 of these left the SME sector. This probably reflects the recruitment policies of the larger businesses in that they probably favour University graduates.

4. Factors That Predict: 'STAYED IN THE NORTH EAST'

Only two factors have any significant bearing on the location of the students six months after the end of the programme. Those that are still in the North East (regardless of whether they are still with the GAP employer):

	Significance
1. Home outside North East, and college in North East	>90%
2. Do not have high leadership indicators	>98%

The first result indicates that students from homes outside the North East, who came to the region for higher education and then stayed for a year on GAP, were more likely to stay in the region. Conversely, those from North East homes who went to colleges elsewhere tend to drift away even after returning to the region for a year for GAP. Of the eight in this category only one stayed in the region for his post-GAP job.

Implications for selection of businesses and graduates

We would improve the retention of graduates in the SMEs if we were to aim for the bigger SMEs and be particularly wary of those of under 20 staff. However this is counter to the objective of assisting such firms to grow by helping them make good use of graduates. Instead we should ensure that the weaker graduates are not placed in very small companies.

The results suggest that if we were to use A-levels, leadership indicators, and degree subject as selection criteria we would improve the success rates as seen by the GAP employer. In addition, giving preference to Polytechnic students, and those from homes outside the North East would improve the retention rates in the SME sector and the North East respectively. The rejection of candidates with good leadership indicators 'goes against the grain' somewhat, but may be justified on the additional grounds that these graduates will do well anyway and the intervention of GAP is more valuable to the others who are bright, but need more personal development.

In the recruitment for GAP5 a scoring system based on all the factors that were statistically significant was used in screening the very large number of applicants. It favoured those with:

1. At least 9 A-level points.
2. Not high leadership indicators.
3. Have studied Engineering or Science.
4. Home not in North East but College in North East.
5. Attended a Polytechnic.

Time will tell whether the 17 graduates on GAP5 prove even more successful than their predecessors.

CONCLUSIONS - DEVELOPMENT OF GAP

With our new understanding of some of the factors that influence the success of GAP, and confidence that it currently meets its objectives we can develop it further into other client areas such as family businesses and very small companies. Both of these bring new and special problems in the areas of working relationships that will require even more emphasis on personal skills.

APPENDIX 5

INVESTORS-IN-PEOPLE

Investors-in-People is managed by Investors-in-People UK* and implemented through the network of Training and Enterprise Councils. Comprehensive information on the national standard and how it is operated is available from the TECs. The section on evaluation shown here is about to be replaced by a new version.

EVALUATING YOUR INVESTMENT IN PEOPLE

WHAT DOES EVALUATION MEAN?

Evaluation can be used as a technical term. Here it means the following.

- Checking that what was supposed to happen did happen.
- Checking that it happened in the way it was supposed to.
- Checking on the impact the investment had on your people, and the impact that the changes to them have had on the business and its customers.
- Checking that continuing investment still adds value to the business.

WHAT NEEDS TO BE EVALUATED?

All training and development done, whether off or on the job, should be measured for its effectiveness (this is sometimes called validation). That means asking trainers, trainees, and their managers the following questions.

- Was it well delivered?
- Did it alter what people do?
- Has the knowledge been used?
- Did it meet the trainees' requirements?
- Did it meet the requirements of line managers?

Off the job courses are often very expensive. But how often do trainers and managers sit down beforehand to agree what they expect the results to be? And how often do they both review the results afterwards?

* Investors-in-People UK, Fourth Floor, 7 - 10 Chandos Street, London W1M 9DE.

Investing in people is about more than individual training courses. The overall investment in training and development probably needs examining.

- Can the business afford the cost?
- Can it afford not to invest?
- What would happen if the budget was reduced?
- What would happen if the budget increased?
- Are the right people being trained?
- Are managers accountable for the money that is being spent?

A very effective way to evaluate is to measure performance against targets. Targets can be set for individuals or for the organisation to meet, or for both. Examples include:

- Is a high proportion of the workforce expressing satisfaction with their jobs and the opportunities they get? Do they have a chance to express a view?
- Are recruitment and retention targets being met?
- Are attendance targets being met? Is absenteeism reducing? How does it match local and sectoral levels?
- Are standards of competence set and met throughout the organisation?

National Vocational Qualifications provide an effective measure for competence. They are now available for most of the workforce. Training and development targets can be set in other areas as well, for example:

- Number of days off the job training per employee.
- Expenditure on training per employee.
- Training budget as percentage of payroll.

But these targets are not themselves enough for evaluation. They can lead to wider development needs being ignored. They relate to inputs, not outcomes. They can lead to training being done for its own sake.

The most difficult, but the most important, part of the evaluation is to identify the impact on the business of investment in people.

- Has quality improved?
- Has productivity improved?
- Have initiative, innovation and self-management improved?
- Has waste reduced?
- Have customer satisfaction and repeat business improved?
- Have the key financial ratios improved (people may make a definite contribution to some ratios like capital investment per employee or added value per employee)?
- Are there public relations benefits from investing in people?

Business improvements will not always be measurable in hard numbers. The enthusiasm of the workforce, the feel of a successful business, and the ability to change quickly, may all stem from the commitment of a business to its people and investment in them. Employee surveys or studies by outsiders may be the only way to evaluate these benefits. The impact on people of investment should not therefore be ignored.

- Are all employees familiar with the aim and vision of the organisation?
- Do they support the aim and vision?
- Can they explain to you, and to your customers, their own job, their responsibilities, who they are accountable to, and for what?
- Can they tell you that their own manager is competent in turn, and is committed to coaching and developing them?
- Are they committed to continuing to develop themselves and the organisation?

WHO DOES THE EVALUATION?

Evaluation is about getting the right results. It is everyone's job. Training specialists, inside or outside the organisation, need to evaluate the effectiveness of what they deliver; does it meet customers' needs? Financial specialists will want to look hard at value for money. But investing effectively in people also means that individual employees, line managers, and decision makers have key roles to play.

Individual employees may well play the main role in evaluating training itself. They will often do this with those who delivered the training, with their line managers, and perhaps with training specialists in their organisations. But the key responsibility to say whether training was useful, well delivered and met expectations lies with individuals. Individual employees can also play an important role in helping you assess the impact of your investment. Having collected information from them, you will have to show that you are acting on the results. That in itself will help to raise commitment and business performance.

Line managers may well play the key role in evaluating progress against training and development targets, and the value of the investment in training and development. They will have a vital interest as well in the evaluation of the outcomes for the business and individuals. They are likely to have the main responsibility for acting on the basis of those outcomes.

Decision makers should play a key role in drawing together the strands of the evaluation, to address these central questions:

- What does this organisation get from its investment in people?
- Is this the most we can get for the least cost?

They will need to look at both budgets and impact. They should not look at costs alone. They should not concern themselves with training in isolation, but should also consider the following aspects.

- Quality strategies.
- Customer expectations and perceptions.
- Effective communication with employees.
- Employee commitment.
- Wider development activity, including management competences.
- Competitors' activity.

Most importantly, they should ensure that effective action is taken on the basis of evaluation. If the business is not getting a return on its investment in people, or it needs a bigger investment, then that must lead to a renewal of commitment and action throughout the organisation.

HOW IS THE EVALUATION TO BE DONE?

Evaluation needs to take place before, during, and after action. In some organisations it will involve everybody for all of the time. Everyone will be continuously learning from their successes and failures, and constantly improving as a result.

That is an ideal. But if you spend all your time evaluating, you may produce less of what customers really want, your goods and services. So some more formal evaluation systems are usually required. They include:

- Simple record keeping, for example of performance and development discussions between managers and individual employees, so that reviews can take place.
- Objective setting at all levels and for all activities, sometimes described as 'Management by Objectives', with performance measured and reviewed at all levels against objectives.
- Evaluation studies of particular events or on-going activities. These are particularly useful if carried out by people with no axe to grind (they could be inside or outside the organisation), but only if recommendations for change are acted upon.
- On-going surveys of activity, showing improvements in performance or performance against a target. Surveys of all staff are particularly valuable, as they ensure that those at the top don't just hear what they want to hear.
- Regular scheduled top-level reviews, that look not just at budgets and spending, but at what people and the organisation are achieving and at what they need to achieve to compete and survive.

DOES AN INVESTOR-IN-PEOPLE DO ALL THIS?

Very few Investors-in-People will do all the things mentioned in the scheme. There are three requirements for meeting the national standard for effective investment in people.

- Individuals, line managers, and those at the top are genuinely involved. That means that they act on evaluation results, they don't just fill out forms or read reports.
- Evaluation looks at the outcomes for people and the organisation, not just at the cost of investing in people.
- Evaluation looks at the impact those outcomes have on the business and individuals. It is not just about the efficiency of the training process.

Employers will choose different ways of meeting this section of the standard, to suit the size of their organisation, its culture, its structure, and the nature of their business.

THE PAYOFF

Any business which evaluates effectively will know the return on its investment in people. It will know that it is getting results. It is making the most of its money. It is doing the things it needs to do to survive and grow. It is delivering what its customers want. It is getting the most from its people.

ADDITIONAL INFORMATION

These three publications provide a good alternative view of the evaluation of training. They are listed in increasing order of complexity and thoroughness.

Truelove, S. (ed) (1992) *Handbook of Training and Development,* Blackwell Publishers, 108 Cowley Road, Oxford OX4 1JF, UK.

Smith, A.J. and Piper J.A. (1990) The Tailor-made Training Maze: A Practitioner's Guide to Evaluation. *Journal of European Industrial Training,* **14**, (8).

Bramley, P. (1991) *Evaluating training effectiveness - translating theory into practice,* McGraw-Hill Book Company (UK) Limited, Shoppenhangers Road, Maidenhead, Berks. SL6 2QL.

The specific aspect of assessment to NVQ standards is covered in the following report:

Twining, J. (ed) (1994) *Competence and Assessment: Compendium No.3, Employment Department's Learning Methods Branch,* Pendragon Press, Papworth Everard, Cambridge CB3 8RG. Telephone: 01480 830345 Fax: 01480 831273

The Industrial Society provide a range of training programmes covering most aspects of training and development. Currently (1994) they offer a two day course 'Training - Evaluating Effectiveness' and a one day seminar 'Evaluation of Training'. Details from The Industrial Society, 49 Calthorpe Road, Edgbaston, Birmingham B15 1TH. Telephone: 0121 452 1030 Fax: 0121 456 3824

The booklet 'Paying for Training' gives details of financial support available for training. It is published by The Planning Exchange, Tontine House, 8 Gordon Street, Glasgow G1 3PL. A new edition is due late 1995.